Glencoe Literature
The Reader's Choice

English Language Coach

High School

McGraw Hill Glencoe

New York, New York   Columbus, Ohio   Chicago, Illinois   Peoria, Illinois   Woodland Hills, California

To the Teacher

English Language Coach is designed to supplement *Glencoe Literature: The Reader's Choice*. It provides classroom teachers with additional options and strategies for guiding English language learners in the regular or mainstream classroom. The materials in *English Language Coach* are intended for students whose first language is not English and who have had some prior instruction in English. *English Language Coach* includes

- several pages of introductory material with information and suggestions to help you understand and effectively work with English language learners;

- a questionnaire to help you determine the English proficiency level of each English language learner in your classroom; and

- worksheets that provide additional practice in the skills and subjects addressed by the English Language Coach activities and notes in the Teacher's Wraparound Edition (TWE) of *Glencoe Literature: The Reader's Choice*.

The worksheets in *English Language Coach* are organized into three sections: Beginning, Intermediate, and Advanced. These sections correspond to the three proficiency levels in English.

The program at your school may include separate ESL classes or "pull-out" instruction, in which English language learners work away from the regular classroom for one or more periods a week. The worksheets in *English Language Coach* may be used successfully in that type of program as well.

 **Glencoe**

The McGraw-Hill Companies

Send all inquiries to:
Glencoe/McGraw-Hill
8787 Orion Place
Columbus, OH 43240-4027

ISBN 10: 0-07-876881-0
ISBN 13: 978-0-07-876881-1

Printed in the United States of America.
2 3 4 5 6 7 8 9 000 12 11 10 09 08 07

Contents

Contents *continued*

Introduction

The English Language Learner Population

The English language learner population is tremendously diverse. The cultures and first languages that a teacher may encounter in the classroom encompass the entire world. Individuals can range from those who have never studied English to those who have attended schools in which English is the medium of all instruction.

Languages Represented

Even though Spanish speakers outnumber other language groups in U.S. classrooms, it is possible that your classroom will have speakers of Haitian French, Croatian, Chinese, or any number of other languages. Some English language learners will have lived in the United States most of their lives. Many others will have arrived only recently.

Educational and Cultural Experiences

The educational and personal backgrounds of your students may also be diverse. Some students will have come from an educational system not unlike our own. Others may have had long and frequent interruptions in schooling. Some students may have experienced personal hardships that most of us cannot begin to comprehend. As a teacher working with English language learners, you will want to be prepared to step back from your own culture and language to view the classroom environment and the literature through the eyes of a non-English-speaking student.

Contributions of Students

Many people unconsciously equate limited language skills with a learning disability. In fact, the opposite is true. Mastering a second language and achieving an understanding of a foreign culture are both admirable accomplishments. A student's lack of proficiency in English should never be associated with any type of learning disability. Learning a second language is not a remedial process. English language learners should at all times be considered as competent as their English-speaking classmates.

The diversity of backgrounds that you are likely to encounter among the English language learners in your classroom can serve as a source of enrichment for all students. The limitless opportunities for cross-cultural comparisons can enhance everyone's experience and understanding. Except for those activities that are specifically geared to language acquisition, every effort should be made to bring English language learners together with English-speaking students. By encouraging cooperation, you promote the sharing of cultures and ideas.

Proficiency Levels

In any class, you can expect a broad range of language-proficiency levels. Grade level is not a measure of how much English a particular student has acquired. An English language learner at grade 8 may have an English-proficiency level identical to that of a student at grade 6 or grade 3. This is in contrast to the rest of the curriculum, where you can assume knowledge built on concepts taught in previous grades.

Beginning English language learners display similar characteristics regardless of age or grade level. It is important to keep in mind that proficiency level in language transcends maturity, social skills, overall sophistication, and (of course) intelligence.

Many practitioners in the field of ESL find it simplest to talk about three levels of proficiency: beginning, intermediate, and advanced. Because the literature, class discussions, and assignments are all tied to academic grade level, you will want to be aware of the language-proficiency levels among the English language learners in your class. The range of proficiencies possible in any classroom makes it crucial that English language learners not simply be regarded as one category or even one group.

Beginning

The beginning ELL student
- has limited or no understanding of English
- rarely uses English for communication except for single words or simple phrases
- responds nonverbally to simple commands, statements, and questions
- constructs meaning primarily from nonprint features
- is able to produce simple written material but with invented spellings, grammatical inaccuracies, and structural and rhetorical patterns from the first language

Intermediate

The intermediate ELL student
- understands more complex speech but requires repetition
- has acquired vocabulary sufficient for dealing with many daily situations
- uses English spontaneously but lacks sufficient vocabulary and structures to express all thoughts
- uses sentences that are comprehensible and appropriate but that still often contain grammatical errors
- generally encounters difficulty comprehending and producing complex structures and academic language
- is able to construct meaning depending on familiarity and prior experience with themes, concepts, genres, and characters
- is most successful constructing meaning when there is background knowledge
- is able to produce more complex, more coherent written material but with a considerable number of errors

Advanced

The advanced ELL student
- is able to read with considerable fluency
- is able to locate specific facts within text
- may have difficulty understanding complex sentence structures, abstract vocabulary, or concepts that are not contextualized
- reads independently but may have comprehension problems
- is able to create written material independently, for personal and academic purposes, with structures, vocabulary, and organization that approach those in the writing of a native speaker

Approaches for Different Language Groups

In general, the more one's first language differs from the new language, the more difficult it will be to master the new language. For example, Cambodian is unrelated to English and has a different alphabet; Russian is related but uses the Cyrillic alphabet; and Spanish is related and uses the same alphabet.

With all language learners, you can expect a certain amount of interference from the first language. Finding out how students' first languages differ from English can help you anticipate and address problems. Discover differences by observing students in class and asking them or their parents a few questions.

The Alphabet

Many students who will need to master a new alphabet will also need to master a new way of reading. A student whose first language is Arabic, Korean, Hmong, or Chinese, for example, must learn a new alphabet and a new directionality in reading.

You will want to ensure every student's thorough familiarity with the English alphabet. Uncover problems by asking the student to write the alphabet in uppercase and lowercase. Then ask the student to say the alphabet or point to letters as you say them.

Also ensure that your student is tracking properly. Ask the student to move his or her hand across the line and down the page while reading. Call attention to and describe mechanics to help your students understand what they need to do differently.

Pronunciation and Spelling

Assume that English language learners will find English spelling and pronunciation difficult. Most languages pronounce one letter one way, but English spelling complicates pronunciation. Seemingly endless vowel and consonant variations can represent some English sounds.

Hearing the new language hastens internalization. Students should be encouraged to listen to audio versions of the literature they read.* Grouping language learners with proficient English speakers will also promote internalization.

Grammar

English language learners inevitably use writing patterns from the first language until they begin to master a new pattern. Older students may be able to set goals for themselves based on identified problems. Younger students are usually better able to mimic what they hear, so repeated and frequent exposure to the patterns of English is most beneficial.

*Audio versions of the selections from *Glencoe Literature: The Reader's Choice* are contained on *Student Works Plus*, a CD-ROM version of each student edition.

English Language Questionnaire

At the start of the session, get as much information as possible about each ELL student from permanent files and previous teachers. Use the questionnaire to conduct an informal interview to learn about proficiency levels and to establish a relationship with the student.

Tips for Using the Questionnaire	
Part 1. If possible, interview the student alone—in a private room, ideally, or in a quiet corner of the classroom. Asking the questions in Part 1 yourself will help you make personal notes on how well the student understands your questions and how fluently the student responds. On a scale of 1–5, for example, you can indicate how well the student understands and responds—information, of course, that goes beyond that provided by the questionnaire.	**Part 2.** The student should complete this section independently. The responses will reveal something about the student's English reading and writing ability. It will also allow the student to talk about his or her concerns about reading in English.

Interpreting Questionnaire Responses	
Part 1. Briefly, most students should be able to understand and respond to a majority of the oral questions. A student who cannot understand or respond is likely to experience significant difficulty participating in class. One who understands and responds but has moderate to serious problems with grammatical structures will need additional classroom support. On the other hand, a student who has reasonably strong listening and speaking skills should be able to participate in classroom discussions. However, oral proficiency—or lack thereof—is not necessarily a measure of reading and writing proficiency.	**Part 2.** Most students should be able to read and respond at least partially to a majority of the questions. A student who is unable to respond to any of the questions is likely to experience significant difficulty reading the literature. A student who understands and responds but has moderate to serious problems with comprehension or responding in writing will need significant classroom support. A student who is able to understand the questions and respond appropriately—though not flawlessly—in writing is probably at a level that will enable the student to read the literature with moderate support.

You can expect a positive correlation between proficiency in both parts and overall use of English.

Part 1: Oral Interview	
1. What is your name? Spell your last name for me, please. Spell your first name, please.	
2. What is today's date?	
3. What is your first language?	
4. What language do you speak at home with your parents?	
5. What language do you speak at home with your brothers and sisters?	
6. What language do you use with your best friend?	
7. What English classes have you taken? Who first taught you English? When?	
8. How long have you been in the United States? Do you like it here?	
9. In what language do you read at home? What do you read at home?	
10. Tell me about yourself. What do you like to do?	

Answer these questions. Read the directions carefully.

1. Write your full name below.

_____

last name   first name   middle initial

2. How long have you studied English? Give details. (Answer in complete sentences.)

_____

_____

3. In the chart below, indicate how well you read and write your first language.
Use the terms very well, a little, and not at all. Then indicate how well you can
understand, speak, read, and write English. Next, add the names of any other
languages you speak. Indicate how well you understand, speak, read, and write
each one.

Knowledge of Languages				
Language	**Understand**	**Speak**	**Read**	**Write**
_____ (first language)				
English				
_____ (other languages)				

4. How much do you read in English? A great deal? Some? None? _____

5. If you read in English, what kinds of things do you read? What do you find most
difficult about reading in English? (Answer in complete sentences.)

_____

_____

6. How much and what kinds of things do you read in your first language?

_____

_____

Language Resources: Thesaurus
Building Vocabulary

A *thesaurus* is a special type of dictionary. It may not always give definitions, but it lists synonyms (words with similar meanings) and sometimes antonyms (words with opposite meanings). Use a thesaurus to help you build your vocabulary. Here is a sample thesaurus entry.

Main Entry: rich

Part of Speech: adjective

Definition: having a lot of money

Synonyms: affluent, prosperous, upscale, wealthy, well-to-do

Antonym: poor

Exercise A Use a thesaurus to help you fill in the entries below.

Main Entry: terror

1. Part of Speech:

_____

2. Definition:

_____

3. Synonyms:

_____

_____

4. Antonyms:

_____

_____

Main Entry: attractive

Part of Speech:

_____

Definition:

_____

Synonyms:

_____

_____

Antonyms:

_____

_____

Exercise B In the space below, write a few sentences about someone or something attractive. Use synonyms for attractive in your sentences.

_____

_____

_____

Context Clues

Determining Meanings of Words

When you read, you may find words that you do not know. Look at the context, or other words in the sentence, to find a clue to the meaning. You can use context clues to figure out the meaning of *abhor* in the following sentence.

The more I read about slavery, the more I was led to abhor and detest it.

Context clue	What it suggests
detest	*abhor* and *detest* are similar in meaning

Exercise A After each sentence, write the context clues that help you understand the meaning of the underlined word.

1. He was a diligent student who always completed his assignments.

_____

2. The motley group of volunteers came from many different backgrounds.

_____

3. His persistence, or stubborn refusal to give up, finally paid off when he found a job.

_____

4. She squandered her money on candy and magazines.

_____

Exercise B Write a sentence for each word, using context clues for the meaning of the word. Then trade papers with a partner and find the context clues your partner used.

diligent_____

_____

motley _____

_____

persistence _____

_____

squandered _____

_____

Multiple-Meaning Words

Homonyms

Multiple-meaning words are words that have several related definitions listed in the dictionary. Sometimes the first meaning that comes to mind when you read a word is not the meaning intended by the writer. That is why knowing about multiple-meaning words is important.

Study the following word web to see different meanings for a common word:

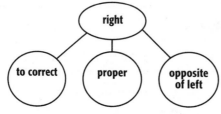

Exercise A Look at the underlined word in each sentence below. Circle the letter of the meaning that fits each sentence.

1. Place the apples on the <u>scale</u> so we can weigh them.

   a. the outer layer of fish and snakes   b. series of steps   c. balance

2. The meat was so <u>tender</u> that the knife cut through it as if it were butter.

   a. not tough   b. offer to   c. kind, loving

3. The salesclerk put the money in the <u>till</u>.

   a. until   b. plow the land   c. drawer of a cash register

Exercise B Read the following pairs of sentences. In each pair, complete the second sentence with a different meaning for the underlined word. Use a dictionary to help you.

1. The boxer <u>reeled</u> backwards under the mighty blow of his opponent.

   To *reel* means to fall back, but it also means _____.

2. The empty lot was full of <u>refuse</u>.

   Refuse is trash, but to *refuse* means to _____.

3. Let's not be <u>rash</u> in making this decision.

   To be *rash* means to be hasty, but a rash is also _____

   .

Synonyms and Antonyms

A *synonym* is a word that has the same, or nearly the same, meaning as another word. To build your vocabulary, make it a practice to learn synonyms for words you already know.

Antonyms are words that have opposite, or nearly opposite, meanings. You also add to your vocabulary when you learn antonyms.

Word	Synonym	Antonym
funny	silly	sad
exciting	thrilling	boring
weak	frail	strong
cowardly	spineless	brave
harsh	cruel	gentle

Exercise A Use a thesaurus to help you complete each sentence. Fill in the blanks with synonyms that fit the context.

1. "Is Bill ill again today?" asked the teacher.

   "Yes he is still _____," answered Mary.

2. Everyone rejoiced at the wedding. In other words,

   everyone _____.

3. After a storm, the air smells fresh and _____.

4. Politely and _____, he asked me to dance.

5. I love to watch her dance because she is so graceful and

   _____.

Exercise B Use a thesaurus to help you fill in the blanks with antonyms that fit the context.

1. He was absent for many days, but now he is _____.
2. One day we rejoiced at a wedding, and the next week we

   _____ the death of a good friend.

3. Outside the air was fresh, but in the flooded basement the air was _____.

4. He politely asked me to dance, but then he _____ turned and walked away.

5. She is very graceful, but her partner is _____.

Analogies: Relationships Between Words

An *analogy* is a comparison that shows a relationship between two sets of things that are otherwise not the same.

The important word in the definition above is *relationship*. To complete an analogy, figure out the relationship in the first pair of words. That relationship should be the same in the second pair of words. For example:

in is to *out* as *hot* is to _____

You know that *in* is the opposite of *out*. Therefore, the opposite of *hot* is needed to complete the analogy. The analogy would be written like this:

in : out :: hot : cold

Exercise A Choose the pair that best completes each analogy.

1. milk : drink ::
   a. little : big   b. hamburger : eat   c. soda : fries
2. chair : sit ::
   a. bed : sleep   b. dog : bark   c. left : right
3. branch : tree ::
   a. much : little   b. red : color   c. room : house
4. brake : stop ::
   a. snow : cold   b. engine : go   c. bird : sky
5. page : book ::
   a. California : U.S.   b. bird : chirp   c. eat : ate

Exercise B The relationship of the words in this analogy is cause and effect.

tired : sleep :: hungry : eat

Fill in the blank with the most appropriate word to complete the following analogies. Use the relationship that is stated before each analogy to help you decide on your answer.

1. **purpose**   story : read :: song : _____

2. **opposite**   stop : start :: win : _____

3. **sequence**   morning : afternoon :: breakfast : _____

4. **likeness**   big : large :: tiny : _____

Denotation and Connotation

Denotation is the meaning of a word as it is defined in a dictionary. It is also called the *literal* meaning.

A *connotation* is a meaning suggested by the word. Connotation refers to a meaning that is in addition to the literal, or dictionary, meaning.

Exercise A With a partner, read each sentence below. Take turns asking questions and answering them. Write the answers on the lines provided.

1. Sentence: Looking up, we saw a kitten <u>dangling</u> from a tree.

   Question: The word *dangling* means "hanging," but what else does it suggest?

   _____

2. Sentence: The officer <u>informed</u> us of our rights.

   Question: If someone informed you of something, do you think that they would speak in a friendly or a formal manner?

   _____

3. Sentence: His heart began <u>racing</u> at the thought of seeing her again.

   Question: When your heart is racing, what kinds of emotions might you be feeling?

   _____

Exercise B Write the definition and a sentence for each word. Use a dictionary to obtain the literal meanings of the words.

dangling

_____

_____

informed

_____

_____

racing

_____

_____

Semantic Slanting

Semantics is the study of word meanings. Semantic slanting is the use of words to influence readers' feelings about a subject. Writers often use semantic slanting in persuasive writing. They choose words with powerful positive (good) or negative (bad) connotations to describe ordinary things. For example, a writer might describe a new breakfast cereal to make shoppers want to buy the product:

New low-fat Crunchy Barola starts a taste riot in your mouth while reducing your risk of heart disease.

Exercise A Read the following pairs of sentences. The first sentence is a neutral sentence. The second sentence of each pair uses semantic slanting. With a partner, underline the words that are positive or negative. Write + or − above each word to show if it is positive (+) or negative (−).

1. A. This program is good.

   B. This gripping drama will touch your heart and forever change the way you think about life.

2. A. The public saw the zoo's new panda for the first time today.

   B. The public flocked to the zoo today to get their first glimpse of the adorable new panda.

3. A. The storm passed over the city.

   B. The storm exploded with wrath upon the helpless city, leaving destruction and mayhem in its path.

Exercise B With a partner, use some of these words to write two sentences about a new television series.

| hilarious   fresh   wacky   edgy   star-studded   must-see   new |

_____

_____

_____

_____

_____

Loaded Words

Recognizing Hyperbole

When a writer uses *hyperbole*, he or she uses exaggeration for effect or to make a point. Look at the following examples of hyperbole.

> *That textbook weighs a ton.*   (Point: That textbook is very heavy.)

> *I could sleep for a year.*   (Point: I am really tired.)

Exercise A Read the following sentences. Each uses hyperbole to make a point. On the lines under each sentence, write the phrase that contains hyperbole. Then, in your own words, explain what point or emphasis the writer is trying to make.

1. That candy bar is hard as a rock.

   _____

   _____

2. When you volunteer for community service, you become a superhero.

   _____

   _____

3. Recycle your glass bottles and save the planet.

   _____

   _____

4. Her explanation is as clear as mud.

   _____

   _____

Exercise B Rewrite each of the following sentences, adding hyperbole to make a point. Then trade papers with a partner. Read each other's sentences and discuss the use of hyperbole.

1. The new girl in class has bright, red hair.

   _____

2. Our star athlete can run very fast.

   _____

3. After lifting weights for six months, my brother has become incredibly strong.

   _____

Word Parts: Roots, Prefixes, and Suffixes

Building on the Base Word

The base of a word may be a complete word or a word part. When the base is a complete word, it is called a base word; when it is a word part, it is called a word root. For example, *teach* is a base word, but *duc* is a word root. You can add prefixes and suffixes to the base word to form new words.

Exercise A Following are base words, prefixes, and suffixes. In the last column, write as many words as you can, using as many of the prefixes and suffixes as possible.

Base Word	Prefix	Suffix	New Words
learn	re-	-er	
press	re-	-ing	
determine	pre-	-ation	
trust	mis-	-ful	
exist	co-	-ence	

Exercise B Add a prefix and suffix to each root below to form a new word.

1. *cept* _____

2. *haust* _____

3. *flect* _____

Word Parts: Suffixes

Using -er to Form Nouns

A *suffix* is added to the end of a word to form a word with a different meaning. When the suffix *–er* or *–or* is added to a verb, it changes the verb into a noun that means "one who does something or makes something." If the verb already ends in *e,* only *-r* needs to be added.

Exercise A Add the suffix *–er*, *–r*, or *–or* to each word. Write the word on the line.

1. drive _____

2. paint _____

3. work _____

4. weave _____

5. act _____

6. farm _____

7. help _____

8. learn _____

Exercise B Use each of the words you listed above in a sentence that shows its meaning.

1. _____

2. _____

3. _____

4. _____

5. _____

6. _____

7. _____

8. _____

Exercise C With a partner, think of five other words with an *–er* or *–or* suffix that means "one who does something or makes something."

_____

_____

Word Parts: Unfamiliar Math and Science Terms

Prefixes That Indicate Number

Many math and science words deal with numbers. Special prefixes are used to show numbers. Some of these common number prefixes and their meanings are listed below.

Prefix	Meaning	Sample Word
deca-	ten	decahedron
kilo-	thousand	kilowatt
tri-	three	trilobite
hexa-	six	hexagram
penta-	five	pentagon

Exercise A Use a dictionary as needed. Write each sample word and its meaning.

1. _____

2. _____

3. _____

4. _____

5. _____

Exercise B Use each of the sample words in a sentence that shows its meaning.

1. _____

2. _____

3. _____

4. _____

5. _____

Word Origins: Etymology

Common Words and Their Origins

Etymology is the study of the origin and history of words. Many common words come from Greek and Latin words.

Exercise A Read the sentences below. Use the clues to help you think of everyday words that come from Greek and Latin. Then use each word in a sentence.

1. The Latin word *diarium* means "daily." What is a book that you write in daily?

   _____

2. The Latin word *sol* means "sun." Our planet is part of what system?

   _____

3. The Latin word *videre* means "to see." What is the name for a tape that you watch on a VCR?

   _____

4. The Latin word part *audio* means "to hear." What is the name for a large hall where people listen to public speakers?

   _____

5. The Greek word part *tele* means "afar." The Greek word part *phone* means "voice." What is the name of the instrument we use for talking to people?

   _____

6. The Latin word *lingua* means "tongue." What is the word that describes the way we communicate with one another?

   _____

Exercise B Read the list of roots below and their original meanings from Greek or Latin. With a partner, write words you know that come from these Greek and Latin parts.

bio, Greek for "life" _____

geo, Greek for "earth" _____

logos, Greek for "word" _____

nov, Latin for "new" _____

astron, Greek for "star" _____

Developing Vocabulary

Defining Compound Words

A *compound word* is made up of two or more words. Sometimes the meaning of the compound word is the same as, or similar to, the meaning of the two separate words.

bath + tub = bathtub (a tub to take a bath in)

Sometimes the compound word has a meaning that seems different from the words that make up the compound.

fire + fly = firefly (an insect)

Exercise A Circle the word that together with the word in boldface makes a compound word. Write the compound word on the line.

1. **lip** mouth stick talk _____

2. **drop** out around by _____

3. **bill** money wallet board _____

4. **out** doors say ramp _____

5. **frost** bite cold snow _____

Exercise B Circle the choice that correctly makes a compound word.

1. frog + man   soon + er

2. place + ment   jelly + fish

3. turn + table   pro + duct

4. sky + scraper   foot + ing

5. fool + ish   scare + crow

Exercise C With a partner, write a sentence for each of the compound words above.

_____

_____

_____

_____

_____

Idioms, Dialect, Slang

An *idiom* is a colorful way of expressing a thought. The meaning of most idioms cannot be understood just by knowing the meanings of the words. Often, context clues can help you understand an idiom's meaning.

Put that in the *circular file.*

We need to *clear the air.*

He'd do well if he ever *cracked a book.*

They're full of *half-baked* ideas.

She has dancing *in her blood.*

Keep this *under your hat.*

Dialect is a way that a particular group speaks.

L'il Abner exclaimed to Daisy Mae, "Yo' sho' are purty!"

Slang is informal language used among friends. For example:

awesome = great   upbeat = feeling good   blue = depressed

Exercise A Complete each sentence by correctly using one of the idioms from above.

1. Here's my idea, but it's a secret. Can you _____?

2. The two feuding sides met to _____.

3. Martin decided he wanted to improve his grades, so he finally _____

_____.

Exercise B Read the following sentences from "The Life You Save May Be Your Own" by Flannery O'Connor. Write in the column what you think the Standard English version of the dialect would be. The first one has been done for you.

Dialect	**Standard English**
1. "That car ain't run in fifteen year," the old woman said.	"That car hasn't run in fifteen years."
2. "I don't know nothing about you," the old woman muttered, irked.	_____ _____
3. "And I wouldn't let no man have her but you because I seen you would do right."	_____ _____ _____

Exercise C With a partner, write three examples of slang that you know and hear at your school. Write what each slang expression means.

Figurative Language: Simile and Metaphor

What's the Difference?

They say that a picture is worth a thousand words. Writers use figurative language to create vivid pictures in readers' minds. A *simile* is a comparison of unlike things using the word *like* or *as*.

- walks like a duck
- looks like a dream
- sighs like the wind

- as strong as an ox
- as straight as an arrow
- as wide as a barn door

A *metaphor* is also a comparison of two unlike things. In this case, though, *like* or *as* is not used.

She is *dynamite* on the basketball court. (She's a good player.)

He is a *walking encyclopedia*. (He knows about many subjects.)

His new car turned out to be a *lemon*. (The car had problems.)

Exercise A Look for comparisons in the following sentences. Underline the two items that are being compared.

1. He's got a brain like a calculator.

2. The cabin by the lake is an icebox at night.

3. My grandmother's computer is a dinosaur.

4. During the exam, time moved as slowly as molasses.

5. Ashlee runs as fast as greased lightning.

Exercise B Which is it? Read all the descriptions of Hector. Label each description *metaphor* or *simile*.

Hector . . .

1. watches you like a hawk. _____

2. has a memory like a sieve. _____

3. is a fierce tiger. _____

4. is a bear when angry. _____

Exercise C With a partner, make up a sentence using a simile and one with a metaphor.

_____

_____

Acronyms and Abbreviations

What's the Difference?

An *acronym* is a word formed from the beginning letters of several words. Look at the following examples:

CD stands for **c**ompact **d**isc.

SONAR comes from **so**und **na**vigation **r**anging

An *abbreviation* is a shortened form of words. Here are some examples:

amt. is a short form of **amount**

atty. means **attorney; Corp.** stands for **Corporation**

Exercise A Write the acronym for the following phrases.

Phrase	Acronym
missing in action	_____
for your information	_____
citizen's band	_____
intelligence quotient	_____

Exercise B Write what each acronym in the chart stands for. You may use a dictionary to help you. The first one has been done for you.

Acronym	What It Stands for
WHO	World Health Organization
NASA	_____
SCUBA	_____
AIDS	_____

Exercise C Write abbreviations to fill in the blanks in the following sentences.

1. Does your train arrive at 3 _____ or at 3 _____?

2. It was time for her annual checkup, so she called to make an appointment with _____ Schiller.

Language Resources: Thesaurus

Precise Meaning

In a *thesaurus*, you will notice that some synonyms are very much alike. Others have slight differences in meaning or connotation.

> **Example:** The word *eat* has many synonyms, but they cannot all be used in place of one another.

Main Entry: eat
Part of Speech: verb
Definition: to take food in through the mouth
Synonyms: bite, consume, devour, dine, lunch, nosh, sup

Exercise A In a thesaurus, find two synonyms for each word below. Write them with their dictionary definitions on the lines.

1. awesome _____

   _____

   _____

2. tell _____

   _____

   _____

Exercise B Write four sentences, using your two synonyms for the words *awesome* and *tell*. Be sure that your sentences convey the subtle differences in meaning between the synonyms.

_____

_____

_____

_____

_____

_____

Context Clues

Determining Meanings of Words

Writers often give clues to the meaning of an unfamiliar word in the sentences around it, or *context*. The chart below shows some types of context clues.

Interpreting Context Clues		
Type of Context Clue	**Clue Words**	**Example**
Definition The meaning of the unfamiliar word is given in the sentence.	that is in other words or which means	All he could do was *gape*, **or** stare, at the accident.
Example The unfamiliar word is explained in familiar examples.	like such as for example for instance	*Fossil fuels*, **such as** coal, natural gas and oil, were formed underground millions of years ago.
Comparison The unfamiliar word is compared with a familiar word or phrase.	too also likewise similarly resembling	Stephen not only *dissembles* at home, but he lies in class too.
Contrast The unfamiliar word is contrasted with a familiar word or phrase.	but on the other hand unlike however	A vulture is a *scavenger*, **unlike** predatory animals, which hunt live prey.

Exercise Read the following passage. On another sheet of paper, record each word, the context clue, and the meaning in this passage.

Mr. Michaels seemed <u>unperturbed</u> by the approaching storm clouds; for example, he laughed and made jokes. Yet he started to set up the tents with great <u>alacrity</u>, or speed. When the storm finally broke, we were all snugly <u>ensconced</u> in our sleeping bags, like hedgehogs in their holes. The <u>din</u>, or noise, of the thunder and lightning was spectacular. In the morning, however, the storm's force seemed <u>ephemeral</u>, unlike the eternal power of the sun, which graced the new day. We all became <u>elated</u> by the cloudless blue sky; for instance, Albert started singing as he made breakfast for everybody.

Multiple-Meaning Words

Homonyms

Homonyms are words that sound alike but have different meanings.

Exercise A Read the passage and notice the underlined words. Then match each word with its meaning in the passage. Use context clues to help you decide which meaning is correct.

Anna made a <u>pear</u> salad for the party. She used a small knife to <u>pare</u> the fruit. Then she placed a <u>pair</u> of candles on the table for a special effect.

1. _____ pear   a. a set of two

2. _____ pare   b. a fruit

3. _____ pair   c. to peel

Exercise B With a partner, find at least one homonym for each of the words below. Write the meanings on the lines below. Use a dictionary if necessary.

right _____

_____

bore _____

_____

beat _____

_____

here_____

_____

to _____

_____

Synonyms and Antonyms

Recognizing Differences in Meaning

A *synonym* is a word that has the same, or nearly the same, meaning as another word.

An *antonym* is a word that has the opposite, or nearly the opposite, meaning as another word.

With a partner, read the poem below and notice how the antonyms show contrasts that carry the main idea.

from "Any Human to Another" by Countee Cullen

The ills I <u>sorrow</u> at
Not me alone
Like an arrow,
<u>Pierce</u> to the marrow,
Through the fat
And past the bone.

Your <u>grief</u> and mine
Must <u>intertwine</u>
Like sea and river
Be <u>fused</u> and <u>mingle</u>,
Diverse yet <u>single</u>,
Forever and forever.

Let no man be so <u>proud</u>
And <u>confident</u>,
To think he is allowed
A little tent
Pitched in a meadow
Of sun and shadow
All his little own.

<u>Joy</u> may be <u>shy</u>, unique,
<u>Friendly</u> to a few,
Sorrow never scorned to speak
To any who
Were <u>false</u> or <u>true</u>.

Exercise A Work with a partner to match the underlined words in the poem that are synonyms and antonyms.

Synonyms		**Antonyms**	
_____	_____	_____	_____
_____	_____	_____	_____
_____	_____	_____	_____
_____	_____	_____	_____

Exercise B Cross out each underlined word in the poem and write a synonym above it. Discuss with your partner how the synonyms change the meaning of the poem.

Exercise C On a separate sheet of paper, write your own poem about joy and sorrow, using antonyms.

Analogies: Relationships Between Words

Kinds of Relationships

Analogies can be based on different kinds of relationships. Some of the most common are shown below.

RELATIONSHIP	EXAMPLE
Part/Whole	hand : arm :: foot : leg
Object/Class	cat : feline :: dog : canine
Antonym	easy : simple :: win : lose
Worker/Tool	artist : paintbrush :: singer : voice
Synonym	small : little :: big : large

Exercise A Make up an analogy that shows the same relationship that is suggested in the following examples.

1. Object/Class   green : color :: pepper : spice :: _____ : _____

2. Synonym   easy : simple :: hard : difficult :: _____ : _____

3. Part/Whole   cells : skin :: bricks : wall :: _____ : _____

4. Person/Vehicle   pilot : plane :: driver : car :: _____ : _____

5. Antonym   up : down :: early : late :: _____ : _____

Exercise B Identify the relationship in each of the following analogies.

1. pot : soup :: griddle : pancakes _____

2. tuna : fish :: pigeon : bird _____

3. thumb : hand :: branch : tree _____

4. artist : painting :: author : writing _____

5. hammer : carpenter :: pen : writer _____

Exercise C Make up two analogies. Identify the type of relationship.

_____ : _____ :: _____ : _____   _____

_____ : _____ :: _____ : _____   _____

Denotation and Connotation

Positive and Negative Connotations

A word's connotation depends on the context in which the word appears or the meaning that the reader brings to it. It may be positive (good) or negative (bad). For example, to *saunter* and to *lope* are synonyms of *to walk* with very different connotations.

Exercise A Decide whether the term in boldfaced type in each sentence has a positive or a negative connotation. Put a plus sign (+) in the blank if the connotation is positive. Use a minus sign (–) if the connotation is negative.

1. ___ For dessert she served a **rich** chocolate pudding.

   ___ To lose some weight, she stopped eating **fattening** treats.

2. ___ My brother **protested** about the poor service in the restaurant.

   ___ The children **whined** when they didn't get what they wanted.

3. ___ Her **straggly** hair needed a comb.

   ___ Today's fashion is long, **wavy** hair.

4. ___ My aunt is a **busybody** who listens in on everyone's conversations.

   ___ My uncle is a **sensitive** person who listens when you speak.

5. ___ The **thoroughbred** horse moved with elegance and grace.

   ___ The **high-strung** horse suddenly reared up and whinnied.

Exercise B For each boldfaced word below, write a synonym, a word that has a similar *literal* meaning (denotation) but suggests a different meaning (connotation). Place a + or – sign in front of each word.

She **ripped** the plant out of the ground.	The steak **sizzled** on the grill.
_____	_____

Exercise C Write a sentence for each word below.

fearful, cautious

1. _____

2. _____

Semantic Slanting

The Appeal of Packaging

Writers use semantic slanting to influence how a reader thinks or feels about something. You will often find semantic slanting in advertising—an entire industry whose sole purpose is to persuade.

An advertiser's job is to make people want to buy certain products or services. Think about food products. What makes them look good? The pictures on the packages look tasty. The words on the package make the product sound good.

Exercise A Look at some common products, such as CDs, sports shoes, video games, jeans, or soft drinks—at home, in a store, or in magazine ads. Work with a partner to fill in the chart, listing words that make these products sound appealing. Then gather information, such as materials, contents, and price, and list those in the third column.

Product	Package/Ad Words and Phrases	Other Information
New CD		
New line of sports shoes		
New video game		
New line of jeans		
New soft drink		

Exercise B Think about a new product you would like to advertise. Name your product, and make a list of words or phrases that you might use to describe it. Use a thesaurus or dictionary to find the synonyms that fit exactly what you want to say. You may wish to make a drawing of your product and add the words you want to appear on the package.

Loaded Words

Recognizing Propaganda

Propaganda is speech, writing, or other attempts to influence ideas or opinions. Many different techniques are used in propaganda. Three propaganda techniques are shown in the chart.

Propaganda Technique	Definition
Testimonial	Famous and admired people praise a product, policy, or course of action, even though they may have no professional knowledge or ability to support their opinions.
Bandwagon	People are urged to follow the crowd ("get on the bandwagon") by buying a product, voting for a candidate, or whatever else the advertiser wants them to do.
Glittering generality	The advertiser uses positive words or phrases, such as *all-American* and *medically proven* to impress people.

Exercise A Underline the part in each of the following sentences that uses a propaganda technique. Then write the name of the technique on the line below each sentence.

1. Join the growing crowd of satisfied customers who bought their mattresses at Nighty-Nite.

   _____

2. This new and improved product has been clinically proven to reduce some symptoms of stress.

   _____

3. Basketball legend Marcus Samson says drinking Desert Bloom Aloe Vera Juice has really improved his game.

   _____

Exercise B Write a sentence using each of the propaganda techniques discussed above. Then exchange papers with a partner. Identify the propaganda technique in each other's sentence.

_____

_____

Word Parts: Roots, Prefixes, and Suffixes

Building on the Base Word

You can add prefixes and suffixes to base words and word roots to form new words.

Exercise Read the prefixes and suffixes and their meanings in the chart below. Then pick words from the word box. Add a prefix or a suffix and write your new words on the lines below. (You may use a word more than once.) After the word, write its meaning.

Prefix	Meaning	Suffix	Meaning
pre-	before	-(i)cal	relating to
counter-	opposite	-ward	direction
ab-	not	-ways	manner
mal-	bad	-ery	establishment
epi-	on, at, besides, after	-(a)tion	state or quality of
anti-	against	-wright	one who works with
uni-	one	-ize	to make
re-	again or back	-al	relating to
un-	the opposite of, not	-ity	state or quality of

Word Box

verse
social
standard
norm
form
center
content
starve
sphere
able
real
out
historic
economic
play
side

1. _____   11. _____

2. _____   12. _____

3. _____   13. _____

4. _____   14. _____

5. _____   15. _____

6. _____   16. _____

7. _____   17. _____

8. _____   18. _____

9. _____   19. _____

10. _____   20. _____

Word Parts: Suffixes

Using Suffixes to Form Nouns

A *suffix* is added to the end of a word to change its meaning or use. The following suffixes form nouns when added to a base word.

Suffix	Meaning	Example
-ant	one who	servant
-dom	state or quality of	freedom
-ess	female	countess
-ette	little one	diskette
-ness	state or quality of	kindness

Exercise A Each of the following words combines a base word and suffix. Write the meaning next to it. Then write a sentence using the word.

1. darkness _____

_____

2. kingdom _____

_____

3. immigrant _____

_____

4. kitchenette _____

_____

5. lioness _____

_____

Exercise B Think of two other nouns that are formed by adding suffixes. Use each word in a sentence. Underline the noun.

1. _____

_____

2. _____

_____

Word Parts: Unfamiliar Math and Science Terms
Prefixes That Indicate Number

When you read math and science texts, you often find words or phrases that are unfamiliar in that context. Sometimes you can guess the meaning because you know the meaning of the word or words in everyday use.

Exercise A Match the words on the left with a definition on the right. Use what you already know about the words to guess their meanings.

1. ____ scale down   a. what a digit is worth within a numeral

2. ____ caret   b. a number that does not change in value

3. ____ constant   c. allowing a user to see stored data in any way

4. ____ face value   d. a reduction according to a fixed ratio

5. ____ random access   e. the apparent worth of something

6. ____ place value   f. a wedge-shaped mark indicating place

Exercise B Read the following science terms. Write your own definition for each term. Then check the term in a dictionary. Write the dictionary definition.

1. nucleus _____

   _____

2. sediment _____

   _____

3. mass _____

   _____

4. symbiosis _____

   _____

5. hybrid _____

   _____

Exercise C Choose three of the science terms above. On another sheet of paper, write a sentence that uses each term.

Word Origins: Etymology

Studying the Origins of Words

Etymology is the study of the origin and history of words. Many dictionaries show the etymology of a word in brackets before or after its definition. Here is a sample dictionary entry with its etymology. Note that the symbol < means "comes from."

> **nostril** (nos' trəl) *n.* [ME *nosethirl*, fr. OE nosthyrl, fr. *nosu* nose + *thȳrel* hole; akin to OE *thruh* through]

The entry indicates that the word *nostril* comes from the Middle English (ME) word *nosethirl*, which comes from the Old English (OE) word *nosthyrl*, which comes from a combination of *nosu*, meaning "nose," and *thȳrel*, meaning "hole." It also indicates that *thȳrel* is related to the Old English word *thurh*, which means "through."

Exercise A Look at the list of base words. Then look at the language that the word originally came from and the original meaning of the word. In the last column, write one word you know that is related to the base word.

Base Words	Original Language	Original Meaning	Related Words
1. *cred*	Latin	trust or believe	_____
2. *demos*	Greek	people	_____
3. *liber*	Latin	free	_____
4. *sacr-*	Latin	sacred	_____
5. *gravis*	Latin	-(a)tion	_____
6. *scāla*	Latin	ladder	_____

Exercise B Write a sentence using a word that is related to each of the base words given. With a partner, discuss how the meaning of the base word is related to the modern meaning of the word.

Developing Vocabulary

Defining Compound Words

A *compound word* is made up of two or more words. It usually reflects the meaning of the two separate words that make up the compound word.

pot + holder = potholder (something to hold a pot with)

Sometimes the compound word has a meaning that seems different from the two words that make up the compound word.

up + scale = upscale (wealthy)

Exercise A Combine two words from each group of four words to make a compound word and write it on the line provided.

1. snake   glide   sand   rattle _____

2. dream   day   think   sleep _____

3. face   head   pain   ache _____

4. copy   write   right   print _____

5. boat   storm   wreck   ship _____

Exercise B Complete each sentence by making a compound word from the words in the box.

push	ware	lord	over
land	under	soft	cover

1. My father is a complete _____ when it comes to chocolate ice cream.

2. I just got some new _____ for my computer.

3. Did you pay this month's rent to the _____?

4. Not one of his friends or family knew that he was an _____ agent.

Exercise C With a partner, write a paragraph and use at least four compound words of your own choice.

_____

_____

_____

_____

Idioms, Dialect, Slang

An *idiom* is an expression that has a different meaning from the literal meaning of the words.

She and I *don't see eye to eye.*   After the game we were *walking on air.*

Tom's act *stole the spotlight.*   We're not *out of the woods* yet.

Mr. Wheeler *gets up with the chickens.*   That coach was *asleep at the wheel.*

Dialect is a type of language spoken in a particular region or by a particular group. It may differ from Standard English pronunciation, vocabulary, or grammar.

"Ver you go now?" my grandmother asked when I reached for my coat.

Slang is informal language used among friends. Slang is not used for formal speech or writing.

I thought the new hairdo was *cool.* (attractive)
After graduation they got *hitched.* (married)

Exercise A Complete the following sentences by using one of the idioms above.

1. The chorus was good, but the tenor _____.

2. The show's backers were _____ because of the good reviews.

3. In order to drive the school bus, she had to _____.

4. Because he was _____, the curtain didn't go up on Act 2.

Exercise B Read the following sentences containing dialect from "The Rockpile" by James Baldwin. Rewrite each sentence using Standard English.

1. "I be back before that. What you all the time got to be so scared for."

_____

_____

2. "No," she said, "you ain't got nothing to worry about."

_____

_____

3. "He went downstairs," said Elizabeth, "where he didn't have no

business to be. . . ."_____

_____

Figurative Language: Simile and Metaphor

Writers use figurative language to create vivid pictures in a reader's mind. A *simile* is a comparison of two unlike things using the word *like* or *as*.

She was as quiet as a mouse.   They fought like cats and dogs.

A *metaphor* is a comparison that does not use *like* or *as*.

Friendship is a blossoming tree.   I could see the wheels of her mind turning.

Exercise A Read the similes. On the lines below, explain the meaning of each comparison. The first example is done for you.

1. Love is like a rose.

   Meaning: Like a rose, love is beautiful. But just as a rose's thorns can hurt you, so can love cause you pain.

2. Life is like a roller coaster.

   Meaning: _____

3. Her answer left him feeling like two cents.

   Meaning: _____

4. The lake was as smooth as glass.

   Meaning: _____

Exercise B Look at the words and phrases in the box. Use them to make five metaphors.

freedom   the ballet dancer   her friendship   crocodile   a kaleidoscope
amusement park   jealousy   lighthouse   a willowy reed   a life raft

_____

_____

_____

_____

_____

Exercise C Think of three things you love and three things you hate. Create similes or metaphors to describe each thing. Trade papers with a partner and read each other's examples of figurative language. Talk about how the use of similes and metaphors can create vivid pictures in a reader's mind.

Acronyms and Abbreviations

An *acronym* is a word that is formed from the beginning letters of a set of words.

> CPA = **c**ertified **p**ublic **a**ccountant
>
> SCUBA = **s**elf-**c**ontained **u**nderwater **b**reathing **a**pparatus

An abbreviation is the shortened form of a word.

> Ave. = Avenue

Exercise A Write the words that each of the following acronyms stand for. If you need help, use a dictionary.

1. TLC _____

2. NBC _____

3. ROTC _____

4. SWAK _____

5. ASAP _____

Exercise B Abbreviations are found all around us. What do these abbreviations mean?

1. tsp _____

2. P.M. _____

3. Fri. _____

4. Dept. _____

5. Pres. _____

Exercise C Make your own chart of acronyms and abbreviations. Tell what each means. You may use acronyms for popular Internet terms.

Acronym/Abbreviation	Stands for

Language Resources: Thesaurus

Choosing Specific Words

A good writer chooses exactly the right words to convey his or her ideas. Notice the differences in the following sentences.

General: She *looked* at the people before *standing* to talk.
Specific: She *surveyed* the crowd before *rising* to speak.

Read how one writer uses specific words.

> And it was cold, not painfully so, but cold enough so that I rubbed my hands and shoved them deep into my pockets, and I hunched my shoulders up and scuffled my feet on the ground. Down in the valley where I was, the earth was that lavender grey of dawn.
>
> —from "Breakfast" by John Steinbeck

When this writer uses *hunched* and *scuffled*, he creates a precise word picture of the way he moved in the cold dawn. The reader can see the way he moved and almost feel the cold.

When you are searching for just the right word to convey what you want to say, a **thesaurus** can help you. The word *thesaurus* comes from the Greek word *thesauros*, which means "treasury." That is exactly what a thesaurus is—a treasury of specific words. Here is a sample thesaurus entry:

Main Entry: lucky
Part of Speech: adjective
Definition: having good fortune; happening by chance
Synonyms: advantageous, auspicious, beneficial, benign, blessed, charmed, favored, happy, hopeful, promising, successful, timely
Antonyms: unfortunate, unlucky, inopportune, untimely

Exercise A Look at the general words below and the differences between them and their more specific synonyms found in a thesaurus. Write a paragraph using as many of the following synonyms as you can to express your ideas.

teach advise, coach, demonstrate, train, tutor
laugh chortle, chuckle, giggle, howl, snicker
watch contemplate, notice, scrutinize, spy, stare
smart adept, astute, brilliant, sassy, shrewd

Exercise B Share your sentences in small groups. Notice the slight differences between the synonyms found in a thesaurus.

Context Clues

Determining Meanings of Unfamiliar Words

You already know that words have more than one meaning and that surrounding words can provide context clues. Your own knowledge and experience can also help clarify the meaning of words. For instance, read this sentence:

The smell of the fresh salty sea air was intoxicating.

From the context clues in the sentence, you should be able to figure out that *intoxicating* can mean "invigorating" or "exhilarating." From your own experience or reading, you might know about the smell of sea air and its uplifting effects.

Exercise A Read the following passage and use context clues and your own knowledge to clarify the meaning of the underlined words. In the middle column of the chart, write what you *think* each word means from the context clues. In the third column, write the dictionary meaning for the word as it is used in the paragraph.

Angelica <u>resigned</u> herself to putting the bankruptcy behind her. She wanted to <u>redress</u> her past mistakes and rebuild her reputation. Today, her business is <u>solvent</u>. But she has not forgotten the <u>gravity</u> of her errors. In fact, I <u>marvel</u> at her new maturity and her willingness to accept responsibility for her own actions.

Word	My Definition	Dictionary Definition
resigned		
redress		
solvent		
gravity		
marvel		

Exercise B Check to see whether your reasoning and the dictionary meanings agree. Write a sentence for each of these words, using the dictionary definition in the chart.

_____

_____

_____

_____

Multiple-Meaning Words

When you come across words that have more than one meaning, use context clues to understand the correct definition.

Exercise A Work with a partner to read the following passage. Notice how the underlined words have more than one meaning. Use the context clues or a dictionary to decide which meaning is correct in this passage. Then list other meanings you know or can find in a dictionary.

They would be on him any <u>minute</u> now. His mind worked frantically. He thought of a native trick he had learned in Uganda. He slid down the tree. He caught hold of a springy young sapling and to it he fastened his hunting knife, with the blade pointing down the trail; with a bit of wild <u>grapevine</u> he tied back the sapling. Then he ran for his life. The <u>hounds</u> raised their voices as they <u>hit</u> the fresh scent. Rainsford knew now how an animal feels at <u>bay</u>.

Word	Meaning in Story	Other Meanings
minute		
grapevine		
hounds		
hit		
bay		

Exercise B The title of this story is "The Most Dangerous Game." Discuss with your partner the two meanings of the word "game." How do both meanings apply to this story? Write your ideas on the lines below.

_____

_____

_____

_____

Synonyms and Antonyms

A *synonym* is a word that has the same, or nearly the same, meaning as another word.

An *antonym* is a word that has the opposite, or nearly the opposite, meaning as another word. Sometimes, antonyms are formed by adding a prefix that means *not*.

For example:

satisfied   **un**satisfied   possible   **im**possible

You can also create an antonym by changing the suffix of a word. For example:

thank**ful**   thank**less**   mind**ful**   mind**less**

With a partner, read the following passage.

from "Of Dry Goods and Black Bow Ties" by Yoshiko Uchida

Although Mr. Shimada was not very tall, he gave the illusion of height because of his erect carriage. He wore a spotless black alpaca suit, an immaculate white shirt, and a white collar so stiff it might have overcome a lesser man. He also wore a black bow tie, black shoes that buttoned up the side and a gold watch whose thick chain looped grandly on his vest. He was probably in his fifties then, a ruddy-faced man whose hair, already turning white, was parted carefully in the center. He was an imposing figure to confront a young man fresh from Japan.

Exercise A Draw a line to match the list of synonyms to words from the passage.

Words from the passage	Synonyms
grandly	upright
erect	immaculate
spotless	impressive
imposing	magnificently

Exercise B Draw a line to match the list of antonyms to words from the passage.

Words from the passage	Antonyms
imposing	carelessly
illusion	humble
grandly	reality
carefully	shabbily

Analogies: Relationships Between Words

Making Vivid Comparisons

Writers often use an analogy to explain an unfamiliar idea by comparing it to something familiar. Writers do this to make their ideas more clear and their writing more vivid.

Exercise A Read the "The Negro Speaks of Rivers" by Langston Hughes. List pairs of things or ideas that are being compared. You may use words in more than one comparison.

> I've known rivers:
> I've known rivers ancient as the world and older than the
>   flow of human blood in human veins
>
> My soul has grown deep like the rivers.
>
> I bathed in the Euphrates when dawns were young.
> I built my hut near the Congo and it lulled me to sleep.
> I looked upon the Nile and raised the pyramids above it.
> I heard the singing of the Mississippi when Abe Lincoln
>   went down to New Orleans, and I've seen its muddy
>   bosom turn all golden in the sunset.
>
> I've known rivers:
> Ancient, dusky rivers.
>
> My soul has grown deep like the rivers.

Comparisons

_____ _____

_____ _____

_____ _____

_____ _____

Exercise B For each pair of words that you listed from the poem, create an analogy.

_____ : _____ :: _____ : _____

_____ : _____ :: _____ : _____

_____ : _____ :: _____ : _____

_____ : _____ :: _____ : _____

Exercise C Trade papers with a partner and discuss the analogies you created.

Denotation and Connotation

The *denotation* of a word is its literal meaning, or its dictionary definition. A word's *connotation* is a meaning that is suggested by it apart from its dictionary meaning.

Exercise In her autobiography "The Story of My Life," Helen Keller describes the arrival of her new teacher, who helped her emerge from her limitations from being deaf, mute, and blind. Read these excerpts.

The afternoon sun penetrated the mass of honeysuckle that covered the porch, and fell on my upturned face. My fingers lingered almost unconsciously on the familiar leaves and blossoms which had just come forth to greet the sweet southern spring.

* * *

Have you ever been at sea in a dense fog, when it seemed as if a tangible, white darkness shut you in, and the great ship, tense and anxious, groped her way toward the shore. . . ?

* * *

As the cool stream gushed over one hand she spelled into the other the word *water*, first slowly, then rapidly. I stood still, my whole attention fixed upon the motions of her fingers. Suddenly

I felt a misty consciousness as of something forgotten—a thrill of returning thought; and somehow the mystery of language was revealed to me. I knew then that "w-a-t-e-r" meant the wonderful, cool something that was flowing over my hand.

* * *

The living word awakened my soul, gave it light, hope, joy, set it free! There were barriers still, it is true, but barriers that could in time be swept away.

* * *

I left the well-house eager to learn. Everything had a name, and each name gave birth to a new thought. As we returned to the house every object which I touched seemed to quiver with life.

The following groups of words appear in the excerpts above. Write the letter that identifies the connotation of each group.

1. ___ My fingers lingered

2. ___ groped her way toward the shore

3. ___ misty consciousness

4. ___ swept away

5. ___ quivered with life

a. She was blindly finding a path.

b. She took the time to sense something.

c. Everything suddenly seems to be alive.

d. The barriers could be easily overcome.

e. Her memory is stirred with vague recollections.

Semantic Slanting

When writers want to influence how a reader thinks or feels about something, they use semantic slanting. They carefully choose words with positive or negative connotations to describe a neutral thing. Writers often use these techniques in advertising and in public service announcements. For example, in a public safety ad, the sentence *Do not skateboard on city streets* could be slanted to read:

Skateboarding on city streets is stupid and reckless and only fools do it.

If you suspect that a piece of writing is slanted, try to paraphrase it by using words that do not have strong positive or negative connotations.

Exercise A Read the following sentences. Each has a slanted message. Rewrite the sentences so that each sentence has a neutral meaning.

1. Save our children's future by voting No on Proposition #1.

   _____

   _____

2. Mentoring a child brings many happy returns—for both of you.

   _____

   _____

3. Make everyone green with envy when you drive by in the sporty new coupe sedan.

   _____

   _____

4. This action-packed movie leaves all the others in the dust.

   _____

   _____

Exercise B Write a neutral sentence for a public service announcement. Then rewrite the sentence with semantic slanting.

   _____

   _____

   _____

   _____

   _____

Loaded Words

Recognizing Bias

Bias is an opinion based on personal preference. In some ways, we are all biased. As a reader, however, ask yourself whether a writer has a bias before accepting everything he or she says. To identify bias, separate statements that are facts from statements that are opinions.

A *fact* is something that can be proven true or false.

An *opinion* is what someone believes to be true.

Exercise A Read the following sentences. Write **fact** or **opinion** beside each sentence. In sentences that contain opinions, underline the word or words that show bias.

1. This morning the mayor proposed a new plan to develop the downtown area. _____

2. The crowd cheered with heartfelt enthusiasm at the mayor's proposal. _____

3. The mayor promised to find the funding for the new development plan. _____

4. The best way to reinvigorate the downtown area is by building new office towers. _____

5. Six high school students interviewed the mayor after the press conference. _____

6. Three students supported the mayor's plan, and three did not.

   _____

7. One student asked the mayor about the skyrocketing cost of building materials. _____

8. It is pointless to worry about unpredictable economic factors.

   _____

9. Only people who are afraid to dream big could oppose this plan.

   _____

10. The planned starting date for construction is September 1, 2007.

    _____

Exercise B On another sheet of paper, write six sentences. In three sentences, state facts. In the other three sentences, express opinions. Trade papers with a partner. Identify each other's sentences that state facts and those that express opinions. Underline the words that show bias in the opinion sentences.

Word Parts: Roots, Prefixes, and Suffixes

Building on Word Roots

If you know the meaning of a word root, you can more easily understand the entire word, even when it has a prefix or a suffix.

Exercise A Read each of the following word roots and its meaning. Then write new words that use the word root plus prefixes or suffixes. Choose from these prefixes: *re-, ex-, sup-, e-*. Choose from this list of suffixes: *-er, -ant, -ent, -late, -tion*.

Word Root	Meaning	Word
claim	shout	
port	opposite	
merge	not	
rupt	break	
vict	conquer	
stimu	against	
volv	roll	

Exercise B Match the words on the left with the definitions on the right. Use a dictionary if necessary.

_____ 1. vagrant   a. motionless, sluggish, dull

_____ 2. stagnant   b. allowing light to show through

_____ 3. epidemic   c. one who wanders

_____ 4. bilateral   d. widespread, found everywhere

_____ 5. translucent   e. prediction of a probable outcome

_____ 6. prognosis   f. having two sides

Exercise C On the lines below, use each of the six words above in a sentence.

_____

_____

_____

_____

_____

_____

Word Parts: Suffixes

A **suffix** is a word part that is added to a word root. Some suffixes change words into nouns.

Exercise A With a partner, use a magazine or newspaper to find words that can become nouns by adding a suffix. One has been done for you.

Root Word	Suffix	Noun
1. desperate	*-ation*	desperation
2.		
3.		
4.		
5.		

Exercise B Use each of the nouns from the last column of the chart in a sentence.

1. _____

2. _____

3. _____

4. _____

5. _____

Exercise C Write a word using each suffix. Then write a definition of the word.

1. –hood _____

_____

2. –kin _____

_____

3. –ee _____

_____

4. –ism _____

_____

5. –arian _____

_____

Word Parts: Unfamiliar Math and Science Terms

When you read math and science texts, you often find unfamiliar words. Knowing the meaning of some prefixes can help you figure out the word. Look at the prefixes and their meanings in the chart.

Prefix	Meaning
derm-	skin
cardio-	heart
hemo-	blood
phot-	light

Exercise A With a partner, use a dictionary to complete the word webs below. Fill the ovals with science terms that use the prefixes.

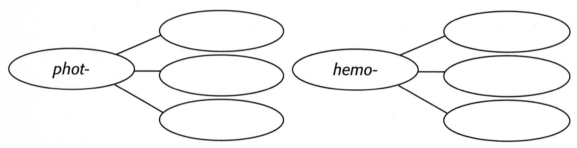

Exercise B Use a dictionary to find the meanings of the six words from your word web.

1. _____

2. _____

3. _____

4. _____

5. _____

6. _____

Exercise C Use two of your words in sentences that show the meanings of the words.

_____

_____

Word Origins: Etymology

If you know the origin and history of certain words—their etymology—it can help you figure out unfamiliar words. Many base words, word roots, and prefixes come from Greek and Latin. Knowing the meanings of these elements is the key to unlocking the meaning of many modern words.

Exercise A In the chart below, read the words and the etymology for each. Use a dictionary to fill in the definition of each word.

Word	Etymology	Definition
benediction	Latin: *bene* (good) + *dictio* (say)	
malediction	Latin: *male* (bad) + dictio (say)	
aquamarine	Latin: *aqua* (water) + marine (sea)	
utopia	Greek: *u* (no) + topos (place)	
misanthrope	Greek: *mis* (hatred) + anthropos (man)	
sympathy	*syn* (like) + *pathos* (suffering)	
philosophy	Greek: *philo* (love) + *sophia* (wisdom)	
antagonism	from Greek: *ant-* (against) + *agon* (contest)	

Exercise B Match the words on the left with the definitions on the right. Use the information in the chart above to help you.

1. _____ aquatic

2. _____ beneficial

3. _____ dictionary

4. _____ anthropology

5. _____ topography

6. _____ philanthropist

a. a reference book of words and their meanings

b. living or growing in, on, or near water

c. a representation of the surface features of a place

d. producing a favorable or good result

e. a person who makes charitable donations for the good of mankind

f. the study of the social development of human beings

Developing Vocabulary

Defining Compound Words

A *compound word*, which is a word made up of two or more words, is often written as one word. Sometimes, however, a compound word may be written as two separate words or as a hyphenated term. The meaning of a compound usually mirrors the meaning of the two parts. Sometimes the meaning is very different.

> homemade = made at home
> mother-in-law = the mother of one's husband or wife
> daddy longlegs = an insect with long, slender legs)

Exercise A Circle the word in each row that will create a compound word when combined with the boldfaced word. Write the word on the line; then write *same* if the word has the same or similar meaning as its parts and *different* if it has an entirely different meaning.

1. **bar**   fall   bell   _____

2. **motor**   lift   car   _____

3. **air**   car   plane   _____

4. **half**   pole   mast   _____

5. **head**   rest   cup   _____

Exercise B On the lines below, write the individual words that make up each compound word. Then write a definition of the compound word, including the part of speech. Use a dictionary as needed.

1. eyelash _____

2. beeline _____

3. statewide _____

4. sunflower _____

5. wristwatch _____

6. folklore _____

7. flashback _____

Idioms, Dialect, Slang

Idioms are phrases that mean something different from the literal meaning of the words. *Dialect* is a form of language used in a particular region or by a particular group of people. *Slang* consists of the informal expressions used between friends.

Exercise A Match each idiom in the left column with the phrase in the right column that has a similar meaning.

1. _____ down in the dumps   a. before something is expected

2. _____ straighten up the house   b. pay any price

3. _____ afraid of her own shadow   c. fearing everything

4. _____ ahead of time   d. feeling sad

5. _____ head in the clouds   e. not being alert

6. _____ give my right arm   f. put away clutter

Exercise B The left column of the chart contains dialect sentences from "The Celebrated Jumping Frog of Calaveras County" by Mark Twain. Rewrite the sentences in Standard English in the right column of the chart.

"The Celebrated Jumping Frog of Calaveras County"	Standard English
He roused up and gave me good-day.	
. . . wife laid very sick once, . . . and it seemed as if they warn't going to save her. . . .	
Smiley was monstrous proud of his frog. . . .	
"Well, I don't see no p'ints about that frog that's any better'n any other frog."	

Exercise C When people get used to the slang meaning of a word, it often becomes the regular meaning. Write the meanings of these slang examples.

1. bling _____   4. phat _____

2. jock _____   5. bonkers _____

3. hip _____   6. nerd _____

Name _____ Date _____ Class _____

Figurative Language: Simile and Metaphor

Figurative language creates pictures in a reader's mind. A *simile* is an example of figurative language that uses the word *like* or *as*.

She eats like a bird.   He's as innocent as a newborn baby.

A *metaphor* is a comparison that does not use *like* or *as*.

He's top banana at his job.   His stomach was a bottomless pit.

Exercise Read these poetry excerpts and describe the similes and metaphors you see.

from "Ars Poetica" by Archibald MacLeish

A poem should be palpable and mute
As a globed fruit. . . .
Silent as the sleeve-worn stone
Of casement ledges where the moss has grown—
A poem should be wordless
As the flight of birds
A poem should be motionless in time
As the moon climbs. . . .

Similes

_____ _____

_____ _____

from "Salvador Late or Early" by Sandra Cisneros

Salvador with eyes the color of caterpillar. . . .

Arturito has dropped the cigar box of crayons, has let go the hundred little fingers of red, green, yellow, blue. . . .

. . . inside that forty-pound body of boy with its geography of scars, its history of hurt, limbs stuffed with feathers and rags, . . . in that cage of the chest where something throbs with both fists and knows only what Salvador knows, inside that body too small to contain the hundred balloons of happiness, the single guitar of grief. . . .

Metaphors

_____ _____

_____ _____

Acronyms and Abbreviations

An *acronym* is a word that is formed from the beginning letters of a set of words. An *abbreviation* is the shortened form of a word or an expression.

Exercise A The postal system requires a specific abbreviation for each state. Write the state after each abbreviation.

AZ _____   WV _____   NM _____   TX _____

VT _____   VA _____   DE _____   LA _____

Exercise B Look at each acronym in the chart and write what it stands for in the next column. Then write four more acronyms and what they mean.

Acronym	Stands For
NATO	
FBI	
HUD	
CNN	
UFO	

Exercise C Look at these common abbreviations. Tell what they mean. Add more common abbreviations that you know.

1. Mr. _____

2. St. _____

3. Dr. _____

4. lieut. _____

5. kg _____

6. misc. _____

7. fig. _____

8. doz. _____

9. _____

10. _____

11. _____

Answers

Answers are provided for those exercises for which specific responses can be anticipated.

PAGE 6 (Language Resources: Thesaurus)
Exercise A
Main Entry: terror
Part of Speech: noun
Definition: overwhelming fear
Synonyms: Answers will vary but may include anxiety, apprehensiveness, jitters, qualm, scare, terror, uneasiness, worry
Antonyms: Answers will vary but may include boldness, bravery, courage, fearlessness, valor
Main Entry: attractive
Part of Speech: adjective
Definition: likable
Synonyms: Answers will vary but may include okay, agreeable, attractive, charming, delightful, genial, good, kind, lovely, pleasant, pleasurable, well-mannered
Antonyms: Answers will vary but may include mean, unlikable, unpleasant

Exercise B
Answers will vary.

PAGE 7 (Context Clues)
Exercise A
1. always completed his assignments
2. many different backgrounds
3. stubborn refusal to give up
4. candy and magazines

Exercise B
Answers will vary.

PAGE 8 (Multiple-Meaning Words)
Exercise A
1. c
2. a
3. c

Exercise B
1. to pull in a fish by winding a line on a reel
2. say no
3. an outbreak of red marks on the skin

PAGE 9 (Synonyms and Antonyms)
Exercise A (possible answers)
1. sick
2. celebrated
3. crisp
4. graciously
5. coordinated

Exercise B
1. present
2. mourned
3. stale
4. rudely
5. clumsy

PAGE 10 (Analogies: Relationships between Words)
Exercise A
1. b
2. a
3. c
4. b
5. a

Exercise B
1. sing
2. lose
3. lunch
4. small

PAGE 11 (Denotation and Connotation)
Exercise A
dangling: helpless
informed: formal
racing: excited

Exercise B
Answers will vary.

PAGE 12 (Semantic Slanting)
Exercise A
1. positive words: gripping, drama, touch, heart, forever, change, life
2. positive words: flocked, glimpse, adorable, new
3. negative: exploded, wrath, helpless, destruction, mayhem

Exercise B
Responses will vary.

PAGE 13 (Loaded Words)
Exercise A
1. hard as a rock; the candy bar is really hard
2. you become a superhero; volunteering for community service is a very important and helpful thing to do
3. save the planet; recycling glass bottles will help the environment
4. as clear as mud; her explanation is not clear at all

Exercise B (possible answers)
1. The new girl in class has hair as red as fire.
2. Our star athlete can run like the wind.
3. My brother could lift a car.
4. My little sister could talk your ears off.

Answers

PAGE 14 (Word Parts: Roots, Prefixes, and Suffixes)
Exercise A
relearn, learner, learnable, repress, pressing, repressing, predetermine, determination, predetermine, predetermination, trustful, mistrust, mistrustful, existence, coexist, coexistence

Exercise B (possible answers)
1. exception
2. exhaustion
3. inflection, reflection, deflection

PAGE 15 (Word Parts: Suffixes)
Exercise A
1. driver
2. painter
3. worker
4. weaver
5. actor
6. farmer
7. helper
8. earner

Exercise B
Answers will vary.

Exercise C
Answers will vary but might include singer, editor, writer, printer, player.

PAGE 16 (Word Parts: Unfamiliar Math and Science Terms)
EXERCISE A
1. decahedron: a solid figure with ten plane surfaces
2. kilowat: a unit of electrical power equal to 1,000 watts
3. trilobite: an extinct arthroped with a body divided into three parts
4. hexagram: a figure having the shape of a six-pointed star
5. pentagon: a polygon of five angles and five sides

Exercise B
Answers will vary.

PAGE 17 (Word Origins: Etymology)
Exercise A
1. diary
2. solar
3. video
4. auditorium
5. telephone
6. language

Exercise B
Answers will vary but might include:
biology, biome, biography
geography, geological, geosphere
logo, logic, logical
novel, novelty, novice, renovate
astronomy, astrology, astronaut

PAGE 18 (Developing Vocabulary)
Exercise A
1. lipstick
2. dropout
3. billboard
4. outdoors
5. frostbite

Exercise B
1. frogman
2. jellyfish
3. turntable
4. skyscraper
5. scarecrow

Exercise C
Answers will vary.

PAGE 19 (Idioms, Dialect, Slang)
Exercise A
1. keep this under your hat?
2. clear the air.
3. cracked a book.

Exercise B
2. "I don't know anything about you."
3. "And I wouldn't let any man have her but you because I see that you would treat her well."

Exercise C
Answers will vary.

PAGE 20 (Figurative Language: Simile and Metaphor)
Exercise A
1. He's got a <u>brain</u> like a <u>calculator</u>.
2. The <u>cabin</u> by the lake is an <u>icebox</u> at night.
3. My grandmother's <u>computer</u> is a <u>dinosaur</u>.
4. During the exam, <u>time</u> moved as slowly as <u>molasses</u>.
5. <u>Ashlee</u> runs as fast as <u>greased lightning</u>.

Exercise B
1. simile
2. simile
3. metaphor
4. metaphor

Exercise C
Answers will vary.

Answers

PAGE 21 (Acronyms and Abbreviations)
Exercise A
MIA
FYI
CB
IQ

Exercise B
National Aeronautics and Space Administration
Self-Contained Underwater Breathing Apparatus
acquired immunodeficiency syndrome

Exercise C
1. A.M., P.M.
2. Dr.

PAGE 22 (Language Resources: Thesaurus)
Exercise A
Awesome synonyms may include astonishing,
awful, beautiful, breathtaking, impressing,
magnificent, stunning, wonderful, wondrous.

Tell synonyms but include announce, authorize,
command, confess, declare, disclose, divulge,
explain, express, inform, mention, proclaim, report,
reveal, speak, state, utter.

Exercise B
Answers will vary.

PAGE 23 (Context Clues)
Exercise
unperturbed: For example, he laughed and made
jokes; unconcerned
alacrity: or speed; quickly
ensconced: like hedgehogs in their holes; nestled,
protected, sheltered, snuggled up
din: or noise; a huge racket
ephemeral: unlike the eternal power of the sun;
fleeting, not lasting very long
elated: For instance, Albert started singing; happy,
exhilarated

PAGE 24 (Multiple-Meaning Words)
Exercise A
1. b.
2. c.
3. a.

Exercise B
Answers will vary.

PAGE 25 (Synonyms and Antonyms)
Exercise A
Synonyms
sorrow—grief
intertwine—mingle
proud—confident
pierce—strike
Antonyms
fused—single
joy—grief
joy—sorrow
shy—friendly
false—true

Exercise B
Answers will vary.

Exercise C
Responses will vary.

PAGE 26 (Analogies: Relationships Between Words)
Exercise A
Answers will vary.

Exercise B (Possible answers)
1. Tool use
2. Animal/Class
3. Part/Whole
4. Worker/Output
5. To

Exercise C
Answers will vary.

PAGE 27 (Denotation and Connotation)
Exercise A
1. rich +; fattening –
2. protested +; whined –
3. straggly –; wavy +
4. busybody -; sensitive +
5. thoroughbred +; high-strung –

Exercise B (Possible answers)
– ripped
+ sizzled

Exercise C
Student responses should indicate an
understanding of negative connotations of *fearful*
and positive connotations of *cautious*.

Answers

PAGE 28 (Semantic Slanting)
Exercise A
Answers will vary.

Exercise B
Answers will vary.

PAGE 29 (Loaded Words)
Exercise A
1. bandwagon: <u>Join the growing crowd of satisfied customers</u>
2. glittering generality: <u>new and improved; clinically proven</u>
3. testimonial: <u>Basketball legend Marcus Samson says (using this product) has really improved his game</u>

Exercise B
Responses will vary.

PAGE 30 (Word Parts: Roots, Prefixes, and Suffixes)
Exercise
Answers will vary, but many include universe, universal, universality, unsocial, antisocial, socialize, standardize, normal, normality, abnormal, abnormality, reform, formal, formality, uniform, uniformity, epicenter, malcontent, starvation, spherical, unable, ability, unreal, realize, reality, realization, outward, prehistoric, economical, replay, playwright, sideways.

PAGE 31 (Word Parts: Suffixes)
Exercise A
Sentences will vary.
1. the state of being dark
2. the state over which a king rules
3. one who immigrates
4. a small kitchen
5. a female lion

Exercise B
Answers will vary.

PAGE 32 (Word Parts: Unfamiliar Math and Science Terms)
Exercise A
1. d
2. f
3. b
4. e
5. c
6. a

Exercise B Responses will vary. Definitions are as follows:
1. nucleus: a central or essential part around which other parts are grouped
2. sediment: material that settles to the bottom of a liquid
3. mass: the physical volume or bulk of a solid body
4. symbiosis: a close relationship between two organisms that may, but does not necessarily, benefit each
5. hybrid: the offspring of genetically dissimilar parents, often produced by breeding plants or animals of different varieties or species

Exercise C
Sentences will vary.

PAGE 33 (Word Origins: Etymology)
Exercise A Answers will vary but could include:
cred: credit, creditor, credible, incredible
demos: democracy, demographics
liber: liberty, liberal
sacr-: sacred, sacrifice, sacrilegious
gravis: gravity, grave
scala: scale, escalator

Exercise B Sentences will vary.

PAGE 34 (Developing Vocabulary)
Exercise A
1. rattlesnake
2. daydream
3. headache
4. copyright
5. shipwreck

Exercise B
1. pushover
2. software
3. landlord
5. undercover

Exercise C
Paragraphs will vary.

PAGE 35 (Idioms, Dialect, Slang)
Exercise A
1. stole the spotlight.
2. walking on air
3. get up with the chickens.
4. asleep at the wheel

Answers

Exercise B
1. "I'll be back before that. Why are you so scared all the time?"
2. "No," she said, "you have nothing to worry about."
3. "He went downstairs," said Elizabeth, "where he had no business to be. . . ."

PAGE 36 (Figurative Use of Language: Simile and Metaphor)

Exercise A The students' interpretations of the meanings will vary but should resemble the following:
2. Life has thrilling highs and terrifying lows.
3. He felt cheap or worthless.
4. The lake was completely still and shining, without a single ripple.

Exercise B Responses may vary but will most likely include:
Freedom is a lighthouse.
The ballet dancer is a willowy reed.
Jealousy is a crocodile.
The amusement park was a kaleidoscope.
Her friendship was a life raft.

Exercise C Responses will vary.

PAGE 37 (Acronyms and Abbreviations)
Exercise A
1. tender loving care
2. National Broadcasting Company
3. Reserve Officer Training Corps
4. sealed with a kiss
5. as soon as possible

Exercise B
1. teaspoon
2. post meridiem
3. Friday
4. Department
5. President

Exercise C
Answers will vary.

PAGE 38 (Language Resources: Thesaurus)
Exercise A
Answers will vary.

Exercise B
Responses will vary.

PAGE 39 (Context Clues)
Exercise A (possible answers)
resigned: accepted; accepted as inevitable
redress: correct; set right, remedy, rectify
solvent: in good financial order; capable of meeting financial obligations
gravity: seriousness or importance
marvel: feel amazed; to feel wonder or astonishment

Exercise B
Answer will vary.

PAGE 40 (Multiple-Meaning Words)
Exercise A
minute: 60 seconds; a tiny amount
grapevine: jungle vegetation; informal transmission of information or gossip
hounds: hunting dogs; annoys or bothers
hit: arrived at; delivered a blow
bay: Cornered; a body of water

Exercise B
Game means an entertaining activity and also animals hunted for food.

PAGE 41 (Synonyms and Antonyms)
Exercise A
grandly—magnificently
erect—upright
spotless—immaculate
imposing—impressive

Exercise B
imposing—humble
illusion—reality
grandly—shabbily
carefully—carelessly

PAGE 42 (Analogies: Relationships Between Words)

Exercise A Answers may vary. Sample answers are given:
rivers/world
rivers/blood
blood/veins
soul/rivers
dawn/young
hut/Congo
Nile/pyramids
singing/Mississippi
Mississippi/New Orleans
muddy/golden

Exercise B Answers will vary.

PAGE 43 (Denotation and Connotation)
Exercise A
1. b
2. a
3. e
4. d
5. c

Answers

Exercise B
Responses will vary.

PAGE 44 (Semantic Slanting)
1. Vote "No" on Proposition #1.
2. Mentor a child.
3. Buy the new coupe sedan.
4. Go see this movie.

Exercise B
Responses will vary.

PAGE 45 (Loaded Words)
Exercise A
1. fact
2. opinion: heartfelt enthusiasm
3. fact
4. opinion: best
5. fact
6. fact
7. fact
8. opinion: pointless
9. opinion: Only people who are afraid to dream big could oppose this plan.
10. fact

Exercise B
Responses will vary.

PAGE 46 (Word Parts: Roots, Prefixes, and Suffixes)
Exercise A
Answers will vary but may include reclaim, exclaim; porter, support, supporter; emerge, emergent, merger; erupt, eruption; evict, eviction; stimulate, stimulation, stimulant; evolve, revolve, revolver.

Exercise B
1. c
2. a
3. d
4. f
5. b
6. e

Exercise C
Answers will vary.

PAGE 47 (Word Parts: Suffixes)
Exercise A
Answers will vary.

Exercise B
Sentences will vary.

Exercise C (possible answers)
1. childhood
2. napkin
3. employee
4. heroism
5. librarian

PAGE 48 (Word Parts: Unfamiliar Math and Science Terms)

Exercise A
Answers might include: photography, photographer, photocopy, photogenic, photosynthesis, photon; hemoglobin, hematology, hemocyte, hemolysis, hemophilia, hemoprotein, hemorrhage

Exercise B
Answers will vary.

Exercise C
Sentences will vary.

PAGE 49 (Word Origins: Etymology)
Exercise A
benediction: *n.* blessing
malediction: *n.* curse
aquamarine: *adj.* turquoise, blue-green
utopia: *n.* an ideally perfect place
misanthrope: *n.* one who hates humankind
sympathy: *n.* mutual understanding or affection
philosophy: *n.* the study of knowledge
antagonism: *n.* hostility

Exercise B
1. b
2. d
3. a
4. f
5. c
6. e

PAGE 50 (Developing Vocabulary)
Exercise A
1. barbell : different
2. motorcar : same
3. airplane: same
4. halfmast : same
5. headrest : same

Exercise B
6. eye + lash *n.* any of the short hairs fringing the edge of the eyelid
7. bee + line *n.* a direct, straight course
8. state + wide *adj.* occurring or extending throughout a state
9. sun + flower *n.* a flower with a tall, coarse stem and large, yellow-rayed flower heads
10. wrist + watch *n.* a watch worn on a band that fastens about the wrist
11. folk + lore *n.* the traditional beliefs, myths, tales, and practices of a people, transmitted orally
12. flash + back *n.* a literary or cinematic device in which an earlier event is inserted into the normal chronological order of a narrative

PAGE 51 (Idioms, Dialect, Slang)

Exercise A
1. d
2. f
3. c
4. a
5. e
6. b

Exercise B
He stood up and greeted me.
. . . wife was very sick once, . . . and it seemed as though they weren't going to save her. . . .
Smiley was very proud of his frog. . . .
"Well, I don't see any points about that frog that are any better than those of any other frog."

Exercise C
1. jewelry
2. athlete
3. fashionable
4. excellent
5. crazy
6. an intellectual, socially inept person

PAGE 52 (Figurative Use of Language: Simile and Metaphor)

Exercise

Similes
A poem should be palpable and mute as a globed fruit
(a poem should be) silent as the stone of moss-grown ledges
A poem should be wordless as a flight of birds
A poem should be motionless in time as the moon climbs

Metaphors
his eyes are the color of caterpillar
the crayons are a hundred little fingers of red, green, yellow, and blue
his body has a geography of scars, history of hurt
his limbs are stuffed with feathers and rags
his heart is something that throbs with both fists
happiness is a hundred balloons that his body is too small to contain
grief is a single guitar

PAGE 53 (Acronyms and Abbreviations)

Exercise A
Arizona
Vermont
West Virginia
Virginia
New Mexico
Delaware
Texas
Louisiana

Exercise B
North American Treaty Organization
Federal Bureau of Investigation
Housing and Urban Development
Cable Network News
Unidentified flying object

Exercise C
1. Mister
2. street or saint
3. doctor
4. lieutenant
5. kilogram or kilograms
6. miscellaneous
7. figure
8. dozen